TRAGEDY AT
BETHNAL GREEN

uncovered editions

TRAGEDY AT BETHNAL GREEN

Report on an Inquiry into the Accident at Bethnal Green Tube Station Shelter

∞∞∞∞

London: The Stationery Office

First published 1945
© Crown Copyright

This abridged edition
© The Stationery Office 1999
Reprinted with permission.

ISBN 0 11 702404 X

A CIP catalogue record for this book is available from
the British Library.

Printed in the UK by Biddles Limited, Guildford, Surrey
J90928   C50   11/99

CONTENTS

uncovered editions are historic official reports into momentous events which have not previously been available in a popular form. The series has been created by researching government archives in the Controller's Library of The Stationery Office in London. The books which have been selected are particularly readable and revealing. Some subjects are familiar to the public but some are unknown and likely to cause considerable interest. Readers are presented with pure history and allowed to form their own opinions.

The accident at the air-raid shelter in Bethnal Green tube station occurred on the 3rd March 1943. For two days the government withheld information about the tragedy in order to prevent word reaching the enemy. Eventually, an inquiry was held in secret, the results of which were published at the end of the war. This is a copy of that report.

PART ONE

∘∞☽◯☾∞∘

THE REPORT

THE REPORT

The Right Honorable
Herbert S. Morrison, M.P.

Sir,
I have the honour to report that in accordance with
your written instruction forwarded to me on the 10th
March, I opened an Inquiry on the 11th March into
the circumstances of an accident at a London tube

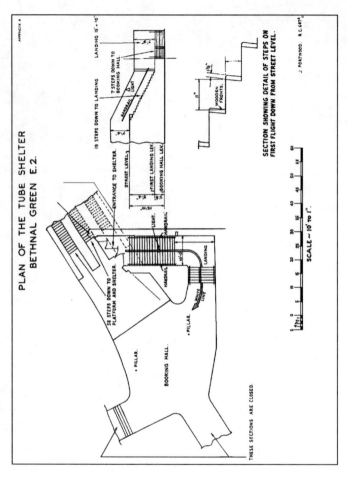

Plan which appeared as Appendix A in the original report.

station shelter, and continued to hear witnesses and others from that date to the 17th March inclusive, with the exception of Sunday, 14th March. Eighty witnesses were examined of whom four were recalled. The following report is the result of that Inquiry.

It will, I think, be convenient to give you at once the more important measurements of the part of the shelter involved. A plan is attached marked "A".

The entrance to the shelter stands in the corner of a public garden on the S.E. corner of the point of intersection of two main roads. There is a church opposite but the general position is somewhat exposed and devoid of cover from adjoining buildings. The entrance, which is the only entrance to the shelter, opens directly off the pavement, which is of some width (10 feet 11inches from building line to edge of kerb). Though the entrance is itself parallel to the line of the kerb, the stairs leading from the entrance into the shelter lie at an angle of about 45° to that line, with the result that the entrance proper is wider than the stairs. While the entrance to the stairs has a total width of some 12 feet 3 inches, the width of the tread of the stairs between handrails is 9 feet 7 inches. The entrance consists of wooden gates opening inwards. A large gate offers an unobstructed ingress of about 9 feet; a small gate alongside, divided from the larger by a wooden upright, has a width of about 3 feet

The wooden gates at the entrance to Bethnal Green tube station air raid shelter.

3 inches. There is a flat concrete sill between the line of the gates and the stairs, on the pavement level. Owing to the angle at which the stairs are set, this is of uneven width. Facing the stairs from a point near the right hand end of the large gate this flat sill is some 3 feet 6 inches in depth to the first tread: from the centre of the small door on the left the depth is 12 feet 4 inches. A flight of 19 steps then descends to a landing, from which a second flight of 6 steps leads at right angles into what would have been the booking hall of the station. The steps of the top flight have a section of 12 inches × 5½ inches and an effective width of 10 feet between the walls. They are plain rough concrete steps with a square wooden insertion on the edge of the tread. They are fairly level though the wooden edge is worn a little below the level of the concrete. The walls of the stairway are wooden with brick piers and support an iron roof. There is a bulkhead light on the ceiling vertically over the 6th step from the bottom. The landing at the bottom is approximately 15 feet × 11 feet. There is a bulkhead light in the ceiling of the landing on a level with the 2nd step from the top of the upper flight of stairs. The vertical interval between pavement and landing level is 8 feet × 2½ inches.

The only lighting of this stair came from a 25 watt lamp in the bulkhead light fixed in the ceiling, which was completely obscured save for a narrow slit of far from clear glass. The cone of the light emitted was adjusted as far as possible to strike the edge of the first step down and to give a dim light over the rest of the stairway. Some reflected light came from the bulkhead fitting over the landing at the bottom. The lighting was extremely dim.

Before describing the accident itself in detail a few general observations may help to make the picture and its setting more clear. The borough in question is almost entirely populated by the working classes. The vast majority of the houses at the opening of hostilities were old, of no structural strength, and offering the minimum of protection against severe bombing. Bombing during the winter 1940–1941 was heavy with widespread damage and the population generally had a severe lesson in the prudence of taking cover during raids. The population at the beginning of the war was in the neighbourhood of 100,000. Through evacuation this has now shrunk to a little over 50,000 despite the return of some adults and a great many children.

The shelter in question was adapted from a tube station in course of construction together with the adjoining sections of tunnel, and was opened early in October, 1940. It has a total bunked accommodation of something over 5,000, with additional shelter for another 5,000. It has only one entrance, though there is an emergency exit some half a mile away in another borough. It was and is the largest single unit of deep shelter in the whole area, and provides a greater proportion of deep shelter per head of population than there is in any of the adjoining boroughs. The shelter population is drawn from the whole surrounding area and people come to it from considerable distances. From its opening it was used by large numbers nightly during the period of intensive bombing, 1940–1941. The use of the shelter became a regular routine and night after night the bulk of the inmates arrived regularly before black out and stayed until the morning. Since the summer of 1941 the regular users have dwindled from some thousands nightly to a mere 200–300. The largest recorded attendance was about 7,000.

On the 16th January, 1943, the papers published an account of a British raid on Berlin. The shelter was used by a fair number of people on the nights succeeding and particularly during the light German reprisal raid on 17th January. It was noticed that a good many people were in the streets in the neighbourhood of the shelter who did not actually use it. On the 28th February 500 people were checked out of the shelter and on the 1st March, 587. News was received on the 2nd March of our heavy raid on Berlin on the 1st, and on that night 850 people actually used the shelter. Again many people were seen in the neighbourhood of the shelter in the streets, obviously up to a late hour prepared to use the shelter if an alert was sounded. The general expectation, however, seems from my inquiries to have been that a reprisal attack was far more likely to be launched on the 3rd.

The state of mind of the people of the area appeared most clearly during my inquiry. They take a most intelligent interest in the accounts of our bombing of the enemy, particularly remembering what they themselves experienced. They did not miss the optimistic accounts in our Press of the results achieved on this occasion, and had noted the changed nature of bombing tactics and the accounts of the results of the ultra-heavy bombs coming into use. The result was that people had made up their minds that in case of an alert it was necessary, or at any rate, wise to get into deep shelter with as little delay as possible. They were a little nervous and apprehensive, though not more so I think than is natural under the circumstances.

On the night of the 3rd March the alert sounded at 8.17 p.m. precisely. By this time it was estimated that about 500–600 people were already in the shelter. The gates had all been opened some time prior to the alert. The chances of a raid were freely discussed but the people were perfectly orderly and normal in the manner of their entry up to the time of the sounding of the alert. Immediately the alert was sounded a large number of people left their homes in the utmost haste for the shelter. A great many were running. Two cinemas at least in the near vicinity disgorged a large number of people and at least 3 omnibuses set down their passengers outside the shelter. From 8.17 and for the next 10 minutes there was a hurried convergence of hundreds of people towards, and at, the gates of the shelter. The people were nervous and anxious to get under cover. The entrance of the shelter was densely packed though there was no actual disorder, and the people were able to enter the shelter in a hurried but orderly stream. As fast as they passed down the stairs, numbers were converging at the entrance behind them. In the 10 minutes succeeding the alert it is estimated that some 1,500 people entered the shelter. A number of these had had advance warning before the actual alert from the fact that their relay wireless had gone off. This, apparently, is a nearly certain sign that an alert will follow. The proportion of women and children was large. At this time there was gunfire, but it was distant and, according to numerous witnesses, not very alarming. No bombs or other missiles had fallen within a radius of some miles of the shelter.

At precisely 8.27 p.m. a salvo of rockets was discharged from a battery some third of a mile away. This caused a great deal of alarm. Some people on their way to the shelter lay down in the road and then ran on. There were some cries reported that "they were starting dropping them": that it was a land mine; and other alarming observations. The crowd surged forward towards the entrance carrying in front of it those who were entering the shelter, and placing a severe and sudden pressure upon the backs of those already descending the nearly dark stairway.

Either as a result of this sudden pressure from behind, or, by an unlucky coincidence simultaneously with the pressure reaching the people immediately behind her, a woman, said to have been holding or leading a child, fell on the third step from the bottom. This was observed both by a witness on the landing below and by at least 2 people in the crowd on the stairs behind her. As a result or, again, simultaneously, a man fell on her left. This occurred in the right hand half of the stairway. So great was the pressure from behind that those impeded by the bodies were forced down on top of them with their heads outwards and towards the landing. In a matter of seconds there was built an immovable and interlaced mass of bodies 5 or 6 or more deep against which the people above and on the stairs continued to be forced by the pressure from behind.

I have not been able to establish definitely whether the woman's fall was fortuitous or caused by pressure. I think there is little doubt that it was the latter. The evidence of a Mrs. Barber who witnessed the fall from behind seems to show that she, Mrs. Barber, had lost her foothold, and was being carried down with her feet off the ground, before the woman fell. In any case the point is a small one and its solution would not throw further light on the causes and origin of the accident.

The people immediately in front of this accident seem to have moved on without realizing that anything had happened. As I have already stated, there is no doubt that they were hurrying to get into the shelter proper. For a very short time, no more than a few seconds, there seems to have been a lane open along the left hand wall. One woman and one woman only escaped from the mass trapped on the stairs and she seems to have been forced along the extreme left. After a few seconds the "jam" was complete across the full width of the stairway.

Returning to what was occurring at the top of the stairs, there was, at the moment when movement forward and into the shelter was arrested, a crowd of about 150–200 outside the shelter and violently anxious to enter it. This crowd was being augmented from minute to minute by fresh arrivals. The immediate effect of the stoppage was to make them press forward harder, and there was an almost instantaneous transition from nervousness and hurry to disorder. There seems to have been an impression among some of the people that they were either being deliberately held back, or that a floodgate situated at the foot of the escalators had been closed against them. I shall deal with this matter later. All the people on the top steps of the stairs were completely unable to move, as were those in the shelter entrance. There were loud cries of distress coming from the staircase, while a good deal of shouting and objurgation was coming from those endeavouring to gain entry. The confusion was rendered worse and confounded by numbers of people who, realizing that something was amiss, were endeavoring to gain access to the stairs to make enquiries after or assist relatives and friends who had preceded them.

Up to this point, which may be taken as some time between 8.27 and 8.28, it is possible to be precise in point of time. Thereafter such precision is impossible and further statements involving time can, except where otherwise stated, be taken as estimates only.

I think it right to point out to anyone reading the transcript of the evidence that it is possible to say that the times given by P.S.'s. Swindells and MacDonald and P.C.'s. Henderson and Stubbington are definitely wrong. We know that no policeman got to the shelter before the trouble, and we know that the trouble started at 8.27 precisely.

The state of affairs outlined above continued for some time; probably until about 8.45. Though the shelter had been passed by a police officer, on his way to report at the station, before the trouble, who was able to give me a clear picture of the state of affairs at that time, it was not until very shortly after the accident that any police officer arrived. He found the crowd out of hand and went towards the station for assistance. He met three other officers on his way and returned at once with two regular officers, sending an auxiliary back for assistance. These officers did the best to control the crowd and clear the mouth of the shelter, but it was not until the arrival of a sergeant and additional constables that this was accomplished, as near as I can judge, at about 8.45 p.m. Though it is not perhaps the proper word to use, there is no doubt that the crowd numbering from 150 to 200 remaining outside the shelter were out of hand and frantic with nervousness, confusion and worry, which heavier gunfire and further salvos of rockets did nothing to allay.

From 8.27 until approximately 8.45 it was impossible from the upper or road side, to get at the serious casualties, which appear to have extended from a point about half way down the stairs to the bottom.

At the shelter end of the stair the position was different, but equally tragic. I should state here that from the booking hall at the bottom of the second flight of 6 stairs escalators with the treads stationary form the stairway to the lower shelter level. There are two escalators, each with a tread width of 3 feet, to take the whole flow of passengers down, and it is the custom the shelter always to have wardens on duty here to prevent loitering blocking of the booking hall, and to assist the aged and infirm down escalators. The flow had been brisk and continuous, and all those examine by me agreed that while the people were hurrying and were talking of expected raid, there was no disorder. There were, or should have been wardens and a helper disposed in posts between the head of the escalators and the main gate, and at the time of the accident all were on the booking hall level. The first notice that the wardens there had that there was trouble, was an interruption of the flow of persons entering the booking hall. Almost simultaneously there were cries and screams from the upper stairway. By the time that any of them had ascended the 6 lower stairs and got to the landing there was already a wall of bodies and their efforts to extricate anyone were futile: they were physically unable to drag out a single body owing to the pressure on them, although it appears that they did succeed in extricating or receiving some 7 or 8 babies. At the time of the accident there was no one on the landing. The nearest person was in fact an elderly man, a Mr. Steadman, who suffers from a weak heart and is allowed to stay in the booking hall. He states that he was near the top of the lower flight of steps on the right and saw the accident happen as I have described.

All efforts to extricate casualties from the stairs from the lower side were unavailing until much later in the evening. A police constable off duty came over the heads of the people from the top to the bottom some little time after the accident but was unable to do any good. Some time shortly after 9 p.m. a chief inspector, a sub-divisional inspector, and 5 constables arrived via the emergency exit, but again were unable to extract casualties from the lower end until the pressure had been to some extent eased from above.

When those capable of moving and most easily moved had been got out from above it was found that the pressure and possibly the pitch of the stairs had produced a strange and terrible result. The bodies of the few still alive and the dead were pressed together into a tangled mass of such complexity that the work of extrication was interminably slow and laborious. This was of course accentuated by the very poor light which could be allowed. The last casualty was not cleared from the stairway until 11.40 p.m.

In giving this account of the actual accident I have not burdened my report with multitudinous references to the statements I extracted at the inquiry. You may, however, rest assured that everything I have set down is amply borne out by the detailed statements to be found in the transcript, and may be accepted as an accurate statement of the facts of the tragedy.

Before dealing with the subsequent events of that night I should like to emphasize the speed with which the situation developed. The statements obtained from some 38 witnesses all confirm this: one only gives an account which suggests the contrary, and his evidence I am in any case, for many reasons, inclined to treat with reserve. The stairway was, in my opinion, converted from a corridor to a charnel house in from 10 to 15 seconds.

With the measures taken to deal with the accident after its occurrence I propose to deal as shortly as possible. Unfortunately the Chief Shelter Warden did not keep a record of the times of messages received or sent out from his post in the shelter. He states he was too busy to do so. I think he should have done so, but however that may be, I can find nothing to suggest that he was remiss or tardy in getting into touch with help outside. He tells me that after getting the first message by telephone from the booking hall he immediately rang up the police, and followed this up with a second message a few minutes later to the effect that assistance was badly needed at the entrance to the shelter. His first message to Control was at 8.40 p.m. precisely. From then on Control took charge of the situation and dealt with the matters of ambulances, rescue parties, etc., while the police were at that time actively engaged in restoring order at the shelter entrance.

The whole of the shelter staff of wardens on duty were at the time of the accident below street level, and I have no doubt did their very utmost to extract casualties. Apart from one woman whom I have already mentioned in paragraph 12, no casualties were dealt with by the qualified nurse on duty in the shelter until after half an hour after the accident, and then only a very few. It appears from her evidence that it was only after the "all clear" at 9.43 p.m. that any real progress was made in getting out casualties from the lower end of the stair. The great majority were in fact removed from the upper level. The nurse was assisted by a doctor, apparently an Asiatic or an African, but I was unable to get into touch with him and I felt in any case that his evidence, if obtained, would carry the matter no further.

Work at the upper level went on uninterruptedly after the entrance had been cleared by the Police. No first aid was attempted on the ground. All live casualties were sent straight to hospitals by relays of ambulances. Dr. Summers, the Divisional Surgeon, arrived on the scene about 9.15 p.m. and took charge after his arrival, but numbers of casualties had already been dealt with by then; I am satisfied that the course adopted was the only practical one in the circumstances and that there was no avoidable delay in dealing with the injured at any stage. I have not seen any other medical man who worked at the scene of the accident but there seems to have been one other qualified man there at some stage besides the gentleman referred to above. In addition to the police, assistance was also rendered by Service men, Home Guards, Wardens and other volunteers.

Ambulance and rescue services directed from Control seem to have worked smoothly and most expeditiously. The first ambulance arrived at the accident about 8.50 p.m. and from then on a constant stream of ambulances was provided until 11.35 p.m. In all, 31 ambulances were called out with 6 light rescue and 2 heavy rescue parties.

I have seen the medical officers who were in charge of the reception of casualties at the different hospitals to which they were dispersed. I can detect no cause for criticism of any arrangements. The first casualties to reach hospital did so at 8.57 p.m.; the last after midnight.

The following particulars concerning casualties may be of interest:

	Dead.	Retained. overnight in hospital	Discharged by 11th March.
Men	27	14	7
Women	84	33	15
Children (under 16)	62	15	8
Total	173	62	30

Of all the casualties examined, that is all the living and some of the dead, only one minor fracture, of the fibula, was discovered.

Death was, in all cases examined, due to suffocation, and the vast majority of cases showed signs of intense compression.

I believe there is only one case of the death occurring of a person admitted living to hospital: all others were cases of bruises and shock with some minor lacerations. Of those rescued alive some were found low down on the stairs and underneath several layers of bodies. Of the 173 fatal casualties 51 were registered for bunks and were regular users of the shelter: 35 were known as regular users of the shelter during air raids, but were not registered for bunks: 87 were either casual or new users of the shelter. The same figures for 45 of the injured persons admitted to hospital would read 8, 6, and 31 respectively.

I have so far made only incidental references to the police arrangements and dispositions on the night in question and I propose now to deal with that aspect a little more fully. From the outbreak of war and during the winter of 1940–1941, when man power had not become such an acute problem as it is to-day, the Division was considerably stronger numerically than it now is. In those days it was possible and the practice to post men permanently on shelter entrances and at the same time maintain sufficient reserves to handle emergencies. The call-up for the Services, particularly during the past year or fifteen months, has caused an appreciable reduction in Police strength and it became absolutely necessary, in order to maintain mobile reserves available at short notice, to make readjustments of beats patrols, and duties. Permanent posts at shelter entrances have in this Division been withdrawn since the summer of 1941, when raiding of the Metropolitan area virtually ceased. It is the fact that no incident has hitherto occurred at shelter entrances in this Division since the first day of war beyond an occasional bit of hooliganism, or quite minor incidents of that description. Actually within an hour of the declaration of war there was a very minor rush for cover at one large commercial building, but this was dealt with without damage or casualties. As a senior officer said to me: "this sort of thing started off as our nightmare – but it never happened."

The system which replaced the permanent allocation of men to particular shelters was to detail men on particular beats nearest to such shelters to go there immediately on an alert. In addition to these posts, patrols and secondary patrols (known as beat patrols) were arranged to secure that a succession of men on patrol passed these shelters during their tour of duty and were so arranged that patrols or beat patrols should always be in reasonable proximity to men posted on the alert to shelter entrances, ready to act should the need arise. Every man in the Division on or off duty had his orders, for his particular duty on an alert being sounded, and the whole experience gained during the war showed that failing something quite exceptional, that system gave perfectly good results.

When the alert sounded, P.C. Henderson, the constable who should have reached this shelter first, was about 660 yards away. He should therefore have been able to get to the shelter entrance within five or six minutes of the alert. In fact he did not do so, and the time at which he estimated his arrival at the shelter both in his statement to his superiors and to me on my first questioning of him, was demonstrably wrong. He did not arrive until after the accident had happened, and that beyond any shadow of doubt was not before 8.27. The same criticism equally applies to the statements of the Station Sergeant and Sergeant Mac-Donald who took a detail to the shelter, as to the times at which men were sent and the times they left the Station. I can find no evidence to suggest that these mistakes in time were anything but *bona fide* mistakes. Henderson, when recalled to try and clear up this point, stated that on his way to the shelter he did have to speak to several people about the promiscuous manner in which they were waving their torches about, and on reconsideration thinks it possible that that may have accounted for some four minutes delay en route. It may be so, but it was certainly unfortunate that on this particular night there was no constable at the shelter for some 10 minutes after the alert, although the police arrangements contemplated a man being in position certainly not later than five minutes previously. As to whether he could have done anything and what, had he been there, it is idle to speculate: the fact remains that he was not there to do anything.

From 8.30 onward I am satisfied that police were despatched to the shelter as rapidly as they became available. Within a few minutes there were a sergeant and 10 constables on the spot and this contingent was further and rapidly increased. By 8.45 an inspector, a sergeant and 15 constables had arrived and thereafter rescue work was organized rapidly and effectively. By about 9.15 there were a Chief Inspector, 2 Sub-Divisional Inspectors, an Inspector and some 60 constables and sergeants at the scene of the accident, and further reserves were not concentrated only because they were not required.

No one would, I should think, suggest that the results of a fairly searching inquiry into police dispositions and arrangements such as a reference to the transcript of evidence will disclose, is fit matter for general publication. I think, however, I may properly state that as a result of such an inquiry, the opinion I have formed is that the Superintendent and his senior subordinates are zealous, experienced and efficient officers, who have organized the policing of the Division along lines which experience had hitherto shown would best combine efficiency with the necessary economy in man power.

It is probably unnecessary to state that police are now on duty nightly at the shelter and will so remain until some further decision is taken.

It will probably be convenient here to make some observations on the inter-related questions that will be on many people's minds: (a) could the police have prevented this disaster, (b) were the police arrangements adequate? To bring a fair mind to bear on these matters one must endeavour to forget for the moment the horror and magnitude of the disaster, and to look at the picture as forming part of a much larger canvas. There are in this divisional area some 59 shelters each holding 200 persons or more. Though even a cursory study would show that in fact the tube shelter was by far the most important shelter in the area, and the most widely used, nevertheless every shelter is a potential danger spot and there are some very large shelters of a different nature in the area. The police of the division have to make such dispositions as will enable them to meet not one emergency, but very possibly several emergencies in the event of air raids, and over a wide area. It is absolutely essential, therefore, that they immobilize

as few men as possible on fixed posts, in order to concentrate and conserve a mobile reserve. But reserves,
while mobile, cannot, except by coincidence, be
assembled to the scene of an emergency which takes
about 15 seconds, at the outside, to develop. It is certain that after the reduction in man power which the
force has undergone the police cannot be expected to
find men on the spot at all points of danger. There are
probably few fields of national effort and production
(with the possible exception of that concerned with
Defence Regulations and their consequential orders)
which have not been affected by man power stringency: the police, like other Services, can only seek to
make the best use of what they have got. I think it
extremely doubtful if this disaster could have been
prevented except by the presence on the spot of a
number of police anticipating, and numerically
adequate to control, a rush by some 450–500 fright-
ened people in the dark. This the police were never in
a position to provide. At the same time it would be
folly not to recognize that even a single tactful and
determined man may often by timely action avert
what a number could not subsequently prevent.
While I have in the past noticed that the appreciation
of certain sections of the population of London for
the Metropolitan Police is occasionally tempered
with a certain reserve, more than one witness before
me showed a touching confidence in the sedative
effect that even one policeman would have had in the
turmoil of that night. That such a man was provided

by the police I have already stated: but by a series of unhappy accidents he was not there in time.

There remains one other question before I leave this part of the Report. Could any steps have been taken by the wardens on duty in the shelter or elsewhere to avert this accident? The wardens service has been very adversely affected by "call-up" both in its quality and quantity. I formed the opinion that in their Controller, Chief Executive Officer, and Chief Warden, the Borough has most competent and conscientious officers and doubtless there are others also, but the rank and file appear to have fallen off both in respect of numbers and physique to such an extent that efficiency is seriously affected. Prior to 29th May, 1942, the permitted strength of the Wardens Service in the borough was 239: at some time prior to that the numbers had been over 300, and were at that level during the winter 1940–1941. On the 29th May, 1942, the number was reduced to 203, and on the 24th June, 1942, to 160. The present strength is 152, and the service has been unable to keep its strength up to the reduced permitted figure. The post in whose area the tube shelter is situated is an amalgamation of two former post areas. It covers 72 streets and used to have a complement of 100 wardens. The present strength consists of 24 full-time wardens and 29 part-time; including the shelter wardens in the different shelters. The tube shelter used to have a staff of a Chief Shelter warden and Deputy and some 12 full-time wardens, besides women wardens.

The muster on the 3rd March in the shelter was the Chief and Deputy Shelter Wardens, 2 wardens on duty in the shelter proper, and 4 wardens posted for duty between the escalators and the street level. Of these one only was a full-time warden. All these 4 wardens are advanced in years and of indifferent physique. The disposition of wardens while the shelter was filling and during the alert on the 3rd March was one man between the main gate and the bottom of the stairs – he was in fact at the bottom of the stairs when the accident happened; two men on duty passing the people from the booking hall down the escalators; and one man on duty near a watertight door close to the office. This man was used by the Chief Shelter Warden or Deputy to take messages or give any assistance required there or elsewhere. He was also in the booking hall at the time of the accident. There were no wardens on duty in the street outside the shelter at the time of the accident. The full-time wardens were all at posts or shelters and the part-time wardens were doubtless proceeding to their air raid positions.

I am satisfied that no act of commission or omission on the part of any of the staff of wardens on the 3rd March was responsible for any part of the disaster, nor in the light of events and in the existing circumstances, could they have done anything to avert it.

I am satisfied that the Chief Shelter Warden, in so disposing of his wardens, made the most effective use of them in the circumstances. The head of the escalators stands out as the vulnerable point in the interior arrangement of the shelter during the time of ingress. It is a bottle-neck: the capacity of the stairs leading to the booking hall is several times greater than the two escalators leading therefrom and he was not only justified in so doing, but obliged to concentrate most of his reduced staff there. Had Mr. Edwards, the warden posted to the main gates and stairs, happened by chance to have been at the right place at the right time, I very much doubt if he was physically capable of dealing sufficiently quickly with the woman who fell: indeed, by the time the press of people immediately in front of this woman had cleared the platform and allowed access to her, it would already, in my opinion, have been too late to do anything. Communication by telephone from the booking hall to the office worked satisfactorily as did telephonic communication between the office and outside.

Before going on to deal, with the main and contributory causes of the disaster I should like at this point
to deal with two specific allegations which have
received some publicity, and which are without any
foundation whatsoever. Each may be dismissed with
a very few words:

≈ That this was a panic induced by Fascists or criminal persons for nefarious purposes. There were some deaths among men with criminal records. They and their relatives are as much entitled to sympathy as any of the other victims. This story had some local, and I hope limited, circulation. It is an absurdity.

≈ That this was a Jewish panic. This canard had a much wider circulation and was, I understand, endorsed by the broadcast utterances of a renegade traitor from Germany. Not only is it without foundation, it is demonstrably false. The Jewish attendance at this shelter was, and is, so small as to constitute a hardly calculable percentage.

Dealing now with the contributory causes of the accident, they may, I think, be conveniently separated into two main groups:

≈ a psychological change in the attitude of the population towards air raids and shelters generally;

and

≈ the physical causes:

The borough has some 60 per cent of its public shelter accommodation in this tube, a much larger proportion than any neighbouring borough. This had instilled in the minds of the people a marked preference for this type of shelter, to the exclusion of more easily reached shelters more widely dispersed. Apart from the regular users, a large number of people not in the immediate vicinity of this shelter had come to regard it as a desirable haven to resort to in the event of what might prove to be a heavy raid.

A particularly strong apprehension of drastic reprisals for the recent heavy raid on Berlin. This apprehension was fostered by newspaper accounts of the effects of new types of bombs.

A realization that new bombing tactics allowed far less time to get under cover than formerly was the case, and that a raid might be expected to reach its maximum intensity in a very short time. In the new type of raid the air raid warning might precede the bombs by a very short margin.

A wholesome respect for the danger from splinters from our new barrage. The mouth of the shelter stands, as I have said, in a somewhat exposed position.

A lack of knowledge of the nature and appearance of the anti-aircraft rockets now in use.

The desire of parents to get their children under cover quickly, which induced numbers of people not hitherto users of the shelter to go there before a threatened raid. A very large number of children have fairly lately returned to the area.

All these factors combined to produce a loss of self control in some hundreds of people attempting to enter the shelter.

The physical presence of large numbers of children who have come back recently to the area retarded the speed of intake into the shelter, and the speed at which people could reach it.

The shelter has only one entrance. In this it is, if not unique, very exceptional in relation to its size.

The lighting on the stairs was very dim, which not only increased the chance of a fall on the stairs, but was bound to produce confusion if one occurred. If a fall occurred, however, no lighting could, in the circumstances of the present disaster, have prevented that happening which did happen.

were no handrails down the centre of the stair-
√. These might have enabled a person falling to
save himself. If such a person was burdened with a
child in arms and a bundle, as many were, their value
would be problematical. If a jam happened despite
their provision, they would almost certainly make
matters worse. As a contributory cause I attach little
importance to their absence.

The absence of a crush barrier, allowing a straight line
of pressure from the crowd seeking entrance to the
people on the stairs. This was, in my opinion, the
main structural defect at the time of the accident.

The main and proximate cause was a sudden rush for
the entrance by probably 350–400 people.

The question as to how far these factors should have
been appreciated by the local authority and provided
against must be a matter for individual opinion. It is
one thing after a "fait accompli" to make a retrospec-
tive analysis such as is contained in this report and that
after an exhausive enquiry into all the matters which
have now thrown light on the position. It is quite
another to be sufficiently prescient to give the proper
values in advance and to take the right action upon
them. A fairly simple inductive process enables one to
realize now that this accident was more likely to happen at this shelter at this time than previously.
Similarly we can say now, that while most of the

factors present here are present in other shelters, it is quite certain that not all of them are to be found in any one other shelter and that therefore it was more probable that this accident should happen at this shelter than at any other.

One must bear in mind that no actual indication of such a disaster had previously been given, and that the physical imperfections of this shelter entrance are exactly reproduced in scores of other tube entrances in the Metropolitan area. This similarity may well have served to obscure the significance of the exceptional feature here, that this was the only entrance into the largest deep shelter in this part of the metropolis. Further it should be remembered that this was not a specially designed shelter. In the circumstances the local authority had to make the best use of what there was: radical alteration was at no time a practical possibility. For myself, I confess surprise that the accident has not happened before, and no one, I think, can exclude the possibility of its happening elsewhere.

During the course of my enquiry I received a number of complaints and suggestions. I propose to set out the nature of those worthy of attention, and some short observations upon each.

≈   That there was no lighting. This is erroneous. There was the lighting I have described in the third paragraph of this report. It was very dim.

This was necessary, as when the gates were opened there was in the existing state of the entrance, no means of black out, and the light rays except for screening were emitted directly from the entrance. In fact the Controller had more than once attempted to give more light by substituting a more powerful bulb and varying the aperture. On each occasion the immediate result was that it was deliberately broken by one of the entrants. The population are peculiarly sensitive to any display of light in an air raid. I could find no evidence that any direct complaint had ever been made to the shelter wardens on this score.

≈ The unequal width of the sill between the line of the gate and the top stair, and alternatively the short interval between gate and stairs. I have no doubt the angle made the first stair a little awkward; but I cannot find that either that or the width of the sill had any effect in the accident.

≈ That there should be additional entrances. Emphatically not: to do so would only increase the potential bottle neck in the booking hall, by making your intake more greatly exceed your capacity to pass people down the escalators.

≈ That there were no handrails. Handrails down each wall had been affixed since April, 1942.

One or two witnesses before me had only noticed the handrail down the left hand side: this may have been due to a trick of the light.

≈ That the stairs were dangerous both in nature and in their obscurity. I have come to the conclusion that falls, though perhaps not actually frequent, were not uncommon. The fallen, old women mostly, seemed to regard these petty misfortunes as something to be expected, and to have been quite satisfied to have their hurts attended to at the shelter aid post without making any complaint. I can find no evidence that any formal or specific complaint was ever made to the shelter wardens, a result which I confess surprises me. I should have expected complaints.

≈ That there were no police at the entrance. Ex post facto this is an obvious form for a complaint to take, but I can find no trace of any demand having been made for police supervision either by the public to the Civil Defence authority or from that authority to the police. There is, of course, much substance in this complaint, which I have already discussed at some length.

≈ That there were no wardens at the entrance. Had there been any, I think they would have been quite useless to prevent this accident. The

Chief Shelter Warden placed such wardens as he had in what were in my opinion the best positions.

≈ That there were no wardens or alternatively that the wardens failed to do anything effective at the bottom of the stairs. The first is untrue and the second is unfair. I am satisfied that the wardens on duty did their utmost to extricate the people on the stairs but were powerless to do so. When the police arrived the position was similar to what it was a few seconds after the accident: they too were unable to get out the fallen until the pressure had been relieved from above.

≈ Inferentially that there is need for strengthening the wardens service. The problem is not peculiar to this borough. In the present man power stringency it is probably insoluble.

≈ That the re-institution of the earlier warning (yellow) would give the police some much needed time to collect reserves and get to raid stations. This is a matter for the consideration of the authorities who alone can properly balance the advantages and disadvantages of such a course. If an earlier intimation could be given to police stations there would appear to be obvious advantages.

I desire now to revert to the question of responsibility, if any, for the disaster on the 3rd March. I should have been content to leave the subject to your consideration very nearly in the shape of my appreciation of the question outlined above, were it not for a matter which I must now lay before you.

On the 20th August, 1941, the Town Clerk, on the instructions of the General Emergency Committee of the Borough, sought authority to incur certain expenditure on work proposed to be done at the entrance of the tube shelter; and to that end, and on that date, sent a letter to the Chief Administrative Officer of London Civil Defence Region enclosing a specification and plan. The relevant item was that the local authority wished to replace with a brick wall the wooden paling or hoarding which then surrounded the shelter stairway, at that time roofless.

After reference to the London Passenger Transport Board, London Regional H.Q. replied to the local authority on the 27th September, disallowing a brick surround to the stairway and suggesting that it could be strengthened with salvaged material.

The borough replied to Regional H.Q. on the 30th September, 1941, and included the following passages which I quote verbatim from their letter.

> "The General Emergency & Finance
> Committee at their meeting yesterday gave
> consideration to your letter of the 27th instant,
> stating that the Regional Commissioners were
> not prepared to approve the scheme for the
> provision of a surround at the entrance to the
> Bethnal Green Tube Shelter.

"The Committee were of the opinion that the Commissioners could not have been in full possession of the facts in arriving at their decision, and I am desired by the Committee to emphasise the circumstances which prompted them to submit their proposal.

"The iron railings of the Bethnal Green Gardens link up with two newly constructed brick pillars at each side of the entrance to the Shelter, and the structure between consists of a double wooden gate and a small wicket gate at the side.

"The Committee are aware, in the light of past experience, that there is a grave possibility that on a sudden renewal of heavy enemy air attack there would be an extremely heavy flow of persons seeking safety in the Tube Shelter, and that the pressure of such a crowd of people would cause the wooden structure to collapse, and a large number would be precipitated down the staircase.

"As the maximum number of persons which could comfortably be accommodated in the Shelter is 5,000, and it is estimated that in a heavy air raid approximately 10,000 people would seek shelter in the Tube, it will readily be gathered that a serious problem would

evolve in the closing of the Shelter to the
excess 4,000 unless some strong means of
preventing their entry is provided.

"It is not unusual for most of the larger shelters
in the Borough to empty into the Tube Shelter
during a heavy attack, and the Committee feel
that there would be the possibility of a serious
incident at the entrance to the Tube if the
responsibility remained with the personnel
alone to prevent the overcrowding of the
Shelter.

"In the light of this further evidence of the
need for the erection of a strong gate to the
entrance, I am directed by the committee to
request that further careful consideration shall
be given to the matter, and that approval will
be granted to the erection of the gate as
suggested.

"I am further directed to add that, in the event
of the proposals being again rejected, the
Committee cannot accept any responsibility
for the consequences which might ensue from
the lack of adequate protection for the entrance
to the Shelter."

As a result of this letter one of the Regional Technical
Advisers inspected the shelter entrance with the then

deputy Borough Surveyor, and reported as follows to
Regional H.Q.:

> "I have again inspected the approach to
> this shelter and I am still of the opinion that
> it would be a waste of money to build up
> a wall round the steps to prevent the crowd
> from forcing their way into the shelter; the
> existing fence with a little stiffening with
> salvaged timber could be made very much
> stronger than the gate. If anything is at all
> likely to be forced it is the gate which I
> agree might be stiffened with advantage.

> "On the other hand the proposal for a covering
> over the entrance, now put forward for the first
> time in the Town Clerk's letter of the 30th
> September, is I consider a necessity since, as
> things are at present during wet weather, rain
> must pour down the approach steps. I strongly
> doubt, however, if anything like 3 inches of
> water could possibly ever collect on the first
> landing even after extremely heavy and
> continuous rain.

> "I have discussed this with the Deputy
> Borough Engineer and he will, I understand,
> submit a proposal for this cover over the
> entrance."

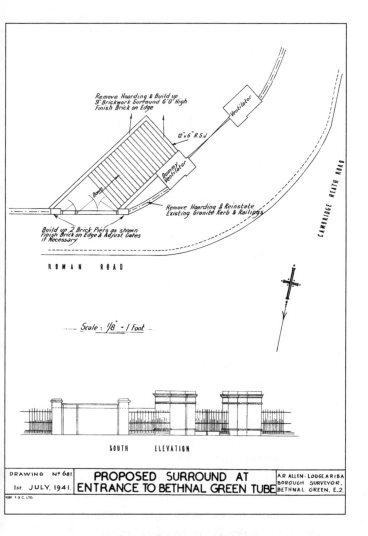

Plan which appeared in the Appendix to the original report.

On the 20th October Regional H.Q. wrote as follows to the Borough:

> "With reference to your letter of the 30th September regarding the surround at the entrance to the Bethnal Green Tube Shelter, I am desired by the Regional Commissioners to say that they have further considered the matter in the light of a recent report by the Regional Technical Adviser, and they remain of the opinion that it is not necessary to remove the existing fencing and replace it by brick walling.
>
> "The Commissioners agree, however, that it is desirable to strengthen the gateway and they also agree to the covering over of the entrance stairway in order to prevent the rain flowing down the stairs into the shelter."

And were answered by letter of the 24th October.

> "Your letter of the 20th instant has been considered by the General Emergency and Finance Committee, and I have to inform you that the Committee remains of the firm opinion that a brick wall surround at the entrance to the Bethnal Green Tube Shelter is necessary.

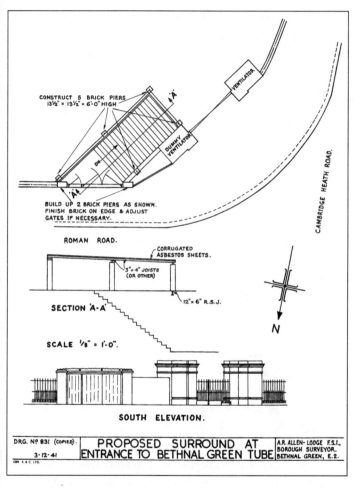

CONSTRUCT 5 BRICK PIERS
13½" × 13½" × 6'-0" HIGH

BUILD UP 2 BRICK PIERS AS SHOWN.
FINISH BRICK ON EDGE & ADJUST
GATES IF NECESSARY.

'A'

DUMMY VENTILATOR

VENTILATOR

CAMBRIDGE HEATH ROAD.

ROMAN ROAD.

CORRUGATED
ASBESTOS SHEETS.

3" × 4" JOISTS
(OR OTHER)

SECTION 'A-A'

12" × 6" R.S.J.

N

SCALE ⅛" = 1'-0".

SOUTH ELEVATION.

| DRG. Nº 831 (COPIED). | PROPOSED SURROUND AT | A.R. ALLEN-LODGE F.S.I., |
| 3-12-41 | ENTRANCE TO BETHNAL GREEN TUBE | BOROUGH SURVEYOR. BETHNAL GREEN, E.2. |

*Plan, showing proposal for covering the entrance, which appeared
in the Appendix to the original report.*

"I am to point out that this facility has been
granted in other Boroughs in similar
circumstances, and to ask that you will be good
enough to reconsider your decision in the
matter."

I think it unnecessary to quote further from the
correspondence, a copy of which is in the Appendix
to this report, together with the relevant plans.

It will thus be seen that as early as August, 1941, the
Borough appear to have contemplated, and to have
presented in unambiguous and clear language, the
very disaster which has so startled and shocked
them now. It is perfectly true that they regarded as
vulnerable a part of the structure whose weakness or
strength would have had no effect on the accident as
it occurred; but they also realized that pressure was
to be expected through the gateway, that is to say,
through the very channel by which it was so disas-
trously exerted on the 3rd March. I attach entirely
secondary importance to the remedies which were
suggested at this stage for the dangers envisaged.
The real significance is that the borough contemplated "a grave possibility of a sudden renewal of
heavy enemy air attack"; that there would be "an
extremely heavy flow of persons seeking safety in
the tube shelter"; "that there would be the possibility of a serious incident at the entrance to the tube
if, etc."

It may be suggested that although the letter of the 30th September appears to raise the "grave possibility" of an accident of the very kind which actually happened, such a possibility was not in fact in the minds of the General Emergency Committee then having the conduct of shelter affairs. Mr. Elsbury, for instance, the Chief Executive Officer of the A.R.P. branch of the Borough Civil Defence, stated that the General Emergency Committee in making such representations did so "merely from a kind of academic point of view." I should find the greatest difficulty in accepting any such contention. That they intended their observations to be taken seriously is the only inference that I can draw from the passage in their letter in which they disclaim responsibility for "the consequences which might ensue from the lack of adequate protection for the entrance to the shelter." When a body in such a responsible position as a Borough is entrusted by statute and moral duty with the task of providing within the resources open to them, adequate protection for their population, they must be taken to mean, and held to abide by, their written word.

I think it was unfortunate, as appears from the answers of the (then) Deputy Borough Engineer, that after the question of the specification to be submitted to Regional H.Q. had been discussed by the General Emergency Committee at whose meetings the Deputy Borough Engineer was present, no members of the General Emergency Committee at any time attended the site with that official to see how he had interpreted their wishes or to discuss with him the problems adumbrated and the solution proposed in his scheme and specification. If the letter of the 30th September properly set out the views of the Committee, and it must be taken so to do, it should have been obvious, I think, that the measures proposed were quite inadequate to deal with the danger which was present to the Committee's mind.

When the Regional Technical Adviser visited the shelter entrance with the Deputy Borough Engineer to consider the latter's proposals, he did so with full knowledge of the contents of the Borough's letter of the 30th September. I am clearly of opinion that that letter, raising as it did certain grave matters concerning an important unit of deep shelter accommodation, should have been treated at Regional Headquarters as something other than a routine application for the expenditure of public funds. Yet that was, in effect, precisely how it was treated. When the Regional Technical Officer visited the site he omitted to consider any of the graver implications of the Borough's letter or to turn his attention to the question how far the Borough Engineer's proposals were adequate to deal with the dangers suggested, the statement of which can fairly be said to have led to his visit. He is perfectly frank in admitting that he would regard it as part of his duties to condemn or criticize proposals which did not seem to meet any particular problem raised. I should find it hard to accept any other interpretation of his duty as an adviser to those he visits. Whether the responsibility for tendering such advice lay on him alone or whether there is any other official at Regional H.Q. whose duty it is to satisfy himself that once such an issue is raised it receives proper attention, I have not considered it necessary to inquire. That seems to me to be purely a matter for Regional Headquarters and ultimately for the Minister, if my view is correct. I regard the omission as unfortunate.

It seems to me to be unnecessary, and beyond the terms of my reference, to attempt to assess at any length the comparative responsibilities of local authorities and Regional Commissioners. That upon the former rests a primary responsibility imposed both by statute, moral duty and common sense is, I think beyond dispute. They, and they alone, by their opportunity for intimate knowledge of their own problems, must be the body responsible for their solution, if that is possible. But it is, I think, quite clear from the nature of the delegation of the Minister's powers to Regional Commissioners, that in clothing them with authority to give directions, there is imposed a duty to give such directions when such directions are necessary, and if and when as in the present case a particular matter is brought to their attention, which from its nature is such that the power to give directions may have to be exercised, there is a duty (quite outside and collateral to the primary duty cast on the local authority) to see that proper advice is tendered when the need for it is shown; and also that if such advice is disregarded, a direction logically follows. Should there be any confusion on this point, there is a danger that the public will fall between two stools. I think the position was quite clearly set out in Home Security Circular No. 133/1940 of the 15th June, 1940, but a lot of paper has rolled over the presses since then, and it may be that a reminder, and if necessary, a clarification of the position, would not now be out of place.

I wish it to be clearly understood that I limit my criticism of the conduct of the General Emergency Committee and of Regional Headquarters to this: that each, a matter of great importance having been raised, failed to see that it was properly understood and considered by their technical officers. It by no means follows that the steps which might have been taken in the light of the experience gained up to that date would have been those now suggested or that they would have been adequate to prevent the accident which has occurred.

During the course of my enquiry a certain volume of criticism was directed to the internal administration of the shelter and in one instance at least, charges of corruption, entirely unsupported by any evidence, were made against the local authority. As to the latter, if they are ever formulated in such a way that a reply is possible, no doubt they will receive attention. As to the former, they can only be brought within the terms of reference to me in so far as they relate to matters which may have contributed to the accident on the 3rd March. One only, I think, merits mention in any detail.

It appears that during the air raid alert on the 17th January the watertight door situated at the foot of the escalators, and giving access to the shelter proper, was closed, or partially closed, while a number of persons were coming down the escalators. The result, though not attended with casualties, did produce a potentially dangerous situation at the time, and there is evidence to show that on the 3rd March some people at the shelter entrance and on the stairs thought that the same thing had happened again. I would recommend that the procedure regulating the opening and closing of this door should be carefully examined and that the most precise orders should be issued on the subject.

While it would be unfair to suggest, from the statements made involving criticism of the administration of this shelter, that the administration was unsatisfactory, evidence that it was noticeably efficient is equally nebulous. The bulk of such criticism came from sources which, however honest in intention, were plainly coloured by political motives and personal animus, and came mainly from persons who for one reason or another had ceased to be employees of the borough authority; but at the same time certain matters, such as the wearing of uniform by wardens on duty, the checking of periods of duty, the recording of messages, and the precise definition and allocation of duties, may have tended to be regarded as automatic rather than requiring constant supervision. I trust, therefore, that I may go outside the strict terms of reference to recommend that the borough authority and the Regional Commissioners should without delay assure themselves that nothing is neglected to secure the highest efficiency in this extremely large and important shelter.

While I am touching on these points may I go one step further. This accident in this particular borough has tended to become an acute point of political controversy. This is most unfortunate and may well lead to an attempt in certain quarters to weaken the position of the borough as the responsible authority. The Chief and Deputy Shelter Wardens are both members of the Council. The allocation of executive positions and offices of profit to elected members of local authorities has been regularised by Section 10 of the Local Government Staffs (War Service) Act of 1939, but none the less I feel that, save in exceptional circumstances, there are strong arguments against such a practice, and it is right, I think, to draw attention to the question.

∞∞∂Q∞∞

In so far as the circumstances of this accident are an index of circumstances to be considered for the future, the steps and modifications taken and made, should afford as effective a safeguard as practical possibilities permit. The entrance to the shelter has been altered to include a covered way leading to the stairs. This will permit of adequate lighting of the stairs and of the approach to them. The stairs have been divided into three lanes by two sets of handrails, and direct pressure into the covered way is controlled and prevented by a crush barrier. A plan of this work is attached and marked "F."

The most outstanding internal weakness of the entrance system is also receiving attention. A third escalator is to be fitted with treads or otherwise adapted to carry passengers. This will diminish the potential bottle neck in the booking hall, and should bring the carrying capacity of this part of the system into line with the capacity of the intake, modified as it will be by the crush barrier.

I have already stated that the police have reinstituted a permanent post at the entrance to the shelter which will be continued until a further decision is taken.

I put forward a suggestion to the Chief Engineer of the Ministry of Home Security, the Chief Executive Officer, the Chief Warden, and the Superintendent of Police, amongst others, which I think may merit consideration. It is that, in those shelters whose nature or length of approach make it of vital necessity, in case of need, to arrest the movement of those in motion in or to the shelter, there should be installed a signal controlled by wardens or those in charge of the shelter, the object of which is to convey to those seeing it that they must stand fast until further instructions. A series of

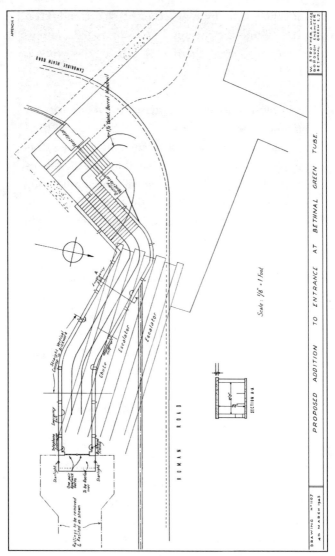

Plan which appeared as Appendix F in the original report.

Workmen installing the hand rails on the stairs.

red lights visible at all points between street and shelter level is the sort of thing I have in mind. Their effectiveness would, of course, depend upon how far their purpose was known to those in a position to see them, and would involve some education of the shelter users. While I make no suggestion that they would prove effective by themselves, they might in certain particular shelters prove a useful auxiliary, and with some diffidence I put forward the suggestion for the consideration of the technical experts.

It would appear prudent, in view of the possibility of a similar situation arising at any large deep shelter to consider the following points:

≈ The possibility of protecting the entrance from direct pressure by a crush barrier. Such a barrier should be sufficiently high to be obvious to persons well back in a crowd. A low barrier cannot be seen and is a grave danger as the crowd may continue to push not realizing the obstruction. It goes without saying that the barrier must be substantial: the pressure which a crowd may exert is enormous. If a rush by a crowd is a possibility, the barrier should be erected at such a point that police can at least deal with the trouble on level ground. No gate can be shut against a press of people. Bostwick or sliding gates may be useful if space is limited, but a solid and obvious barrier wall is almost certainly the most satisfactory.

≈ Entrances should where possible be so screened that stairways and the like can be properly lighted.

≈ The provision of handrails should at least be considered. In a lighted way they should be a help.

May I conclude with two short propositions?

≈ This disaster was caused by a number of people losing their self control at a particularly unfortunate place and time.

≈ No forethought in the matter of structural design or practicable police supervision can be any real safeguard against the effects of a loss of self control by a crowd. The surest protection must always be that self control and practical common sense, the display of which has hitherto prevented the people of this country being the victims of countless similar disasters.

I should like to thank the Mayor and Town Clerk of the Borough for their kindness and for the excellent arrangements made for the holding of this Inquiry. I should like also to thank Superintendent Hill for the most efficient way in which he arranged for the attendance of large numbers of witnesses at extremely short notice, and greatly expedited the hearing. Mr. I. Macdonald Ross, who acted as Secretary to the Inquiry, conducted all the arrangements most admirably, and I am deeply indebted to him not only for them but also for valuable suggestions as to, and information for the purposes of, this Report.

I am,

Sir,

Your obedient Servant,

L.R. DUNNE.

23rd March, 1943.

PART TWO

∞∞OΩOo∞

APPENDIX

Correspondence referred to in the Report

METROPOLITAN BOROUGH OF BETHNAL GREEN

Town Clerk's Office,
Town Hall,
Bethnal Green, E.2.
20th August, 1941.

Sir,

Bethnal Green Tube Shelter – Surround at Entrance

The General Emergency and Finance Committee of the Council at their meeting on Monday last, had before them a plan, specification, and estimate prepared by the Borough Engineer, Architect and Surveyor, amounting to £88 8s. 9d. for the removal of the boarding and the construction of brick wall and piers, re-erection of railings and hanging of gates at the entrance to the Tube Shelter. I enclose copy of the specification, estimate and plan in respect of the work: a copy of the plan has been forwarded to the London Passenger Transport Board for approval.

I am directed by the Committee to request that you be good enough to approve the execution of the above work, expenditure incurred thereon to rank for reimbursement.

I am, Sir,
Your obedient Servant,
(Sgd.) S. P. FERDINANDO.

Town Clerk.

The Chief Administrative Officer,
London Civil Defence Region,
P.O. Box No. 501,
S.W.1.

METROPOLITAN BOROUGH OF BETHNAL GREEN

Specification of work required to be done and materials to be used in forming surround at Entrance to Bethnal Green Tube Shelter

A. R. Allen Lodge,
Borough Engineer, Architect and Surveyors Dept.,
Bethnal Green Borough Council,
Town Hall, E.2.

Remove all hoarding and cart to Columbia Market, Columbia Road, E.2.

Excavate for and lay 6.3.1 Portland Cement Concrete to foundations.

Build in English bond brick walls as shown in Red Rustic brickwork, to match existing Ventilator Piers in Portland Cement 1 to 3 Finish faces of walls fair face with neat flush joint in Cement mortar, and lay damp proof course 6 in. above pavement level. Finish top of work with brick on edge Coping.

Reinstate existing Granite Kerb as shown and set in Portland Cement.

Resite existing railings as shown, tooth into brickwork and let in ends to Granite kerb and run in with lead.

Repair gates, supply and fix special hinges, fixed and hang to piers as shown.

BETHNAL GREEN TUBE SHELTER

Estimate for Constructing brick surround to Entrance

Yds	Ft.	No.	Description	Rate s.	d.	£	s.	d.
	54	Run	Remove hoarding and cart to Columbia Market, Columbia Road.	1	0	2	14	0
	8½	Cube	Excavate and lay Portland Cement concrete foundation 9 in. deep to Piers	40	0	17	0	0
	36	Sup	13½ in. Red Rustic brickwork Piers including pointing and brick on edge Coping.	5	0	9	0	0
	240	Sup	9 in. Red Rustic brickwork fair face both sides	3	6	42	0	0
	44	Run	Lay damp proof course of "Ledkor" of approved material 6 in. above pavement level, include all cutting.	1	0	2	4	0
	10	Run	Relay Granite kerb and set Railings	5	0	2	10	0
			Repair Gates, supply and fix special Hinges, fix and hang.			5	0	0
						80	8	0
			Contingencies, 10 per cent.			8	0	9
						88	8	9

ESTIMATE say £89 0 0

Borough Engineer, Architect and Surveyor's Dept.,
Town Hall,
Bethnal Green, E.2.
July 10th, 1941.

Copy of letter from Regional Technical Adviser to
London Passenger Transport Board

BETH/36   *27th August, 1941.*

Bethnal Green Tube Station; Public Air Raid Shelter

I am informed that the Town Clerk, Bethnal Green,
has submitted to you a plan of a proposal for the
removal of the existing hoarding round the entrance
to the tube and the construction of a brick wall and
piers and re-erection of the railings and gates, etc.
I shall be much obliged if you will favour me with
your observations on this proposal; is it necessary; has
it your approval; would the work be done by you or
by the Borough Council and will this work if erected
all have to be removed when you start running and
would a more temporary form of protection be more
suitable.

The Chief Engineer (Civil),
    London Passenger Transport Board,
    55, Broadway, S.W.1.

Copy of memorandum by Regional Technical
Adviser

BETH/36
RTA/BETH. T.S./AC.

G. BRANCH

Bethnal Green Tube Station Shelter
Construction of an enclosure wall round the
entrance

Reference letter, dated the 20th August, from the
Town Clerk to the Chief Administrator, I have
inspected the site and do not think that a permanent
wall of this nature is required here. I also understand
from the London Passenger Transport Board that this
wall is not required by them and could only be
retained for the war. Under the circumstances I think
that the present hoarding may be allowed to remain.
If the Council are at all nervous about the strength of
the hoarding, it might be strengthened by means of
salvaged timber.

Regional Technical Adviser.

15th September, 1941.

Copy of London Region reply to Borough Council

Exhibition Road.
27th September, 1941.

BETH/36

With reference to your letter (B/S) of the 20th August regarding the surround at the entrance to the Bethnal Green Tube Shelter, I am desired by the Regional Commissioners to say that they are advised that there is no necessity for the removal of the hoarding and for its replacement by brick wall and piers. In the circumstances it is considered that the hoarding can remain, but if the Council have any doubts as to its safety it could be strengthened by means of salvaged material.

The Town Clerk,
    Metropolitan Borough of Bethnal Green,
    Town Hall,
    Cambridge Heath Road, E.2.

METROPOLITAN BOROUGH OF BETHNAL GREEN

Town Clerk's Office,

BETH/36

Town Hall,
Bethnal Green, E.2.
30th September, 1941.

Sir,

Bethnal Green Tube Shelter – Surround at Entrance

The General Emergency and Finance Committee at their meeting yesterday gave consideration to your letter of the 27th instant, stating that the Regional Commissioners were not prepared to approve the scheme for the provision of a surround at the entrance to the Bethnal Green Tube Shelter.

The Committee were of the opinion that the Commissioners could not have been in full possession of the facts in arriving at their decision, and I am desired by the Committee to emphasise the circumstances which prompted them to submit their proposal.

The iron railings of the Bethnal Green Gardens link up with two newly constructed brick pillars at each side of the entrance to the Shelter, and the structure between consists of a double wooden gate and a small wicket gate at the side.

The Committee are aware, in the light of past experience, that there is a grave possibility that, on a sudden renewal of heavy enemy air attack, there would be an extremely heavy flow of persons seeking safety in the Tube Shelter, and that the pressure of such a crowd of people would cause the wooden structure to collapse, and a large number would be precipitated down the staircase.

As the maximum number of persons which could comfortably be accommodated in the Shelter is 5,000, and it is estimated that in a heavy air raid approximately 10,000 people would seek shelter in the Tube, it will readily be gathered that a serious problem would evolve in the closing of the Shelter to the excess 4,000 unless some strong means of preventing their entry is provided.

It is not unusual for most of the larger shelters in the Borough to empty into the Tube Shelter during a heavy attack, and the Committee feel that there would be the possibility of a serious incident at the entrance to the Tube if the responsibility remained with the personnel alone to prevent the overcrowding of the Shelter.

In the light of this further evidence of the need for the erection of a strong gate to the entrance, I am directed by the Committee to request that further careful consideration shall be given to the matter, and that approval will be granted; to the erection of the gate as suggested.

I am further directed to add that, in the event of the proposals being again rejected, the Committee cannot accept any responsibility for the consequences which might ensue from the lack of adequate protection for the entrance to the Shelter.

While discussing the above problem, the Committee also gave consideration to the need for the prevention of the flooding of the entrance by rainwater, and it was pointed out that during a recent rainy period the landing at the foot of the first staircase was flooded to a depth of 3 in. and rain was flowing down to the Shelter.

The Committee agreed to a suggestion that a covering be erected over the entrance to the Tube.

I shall be glad if you will be good enough to approve the scheme in principle and sanction expenditure incurred thereon to rank for reimbursement in full. An estimate of the cost of the roofing is being prepared and will be forwarded to you at the earliest possible moment.

> I am, Sir,
> Your obedient Servant,
> (Sgd.) S. P. FERDINANDO.

The Chief Administrative Officer,
    London Civil Defence Region,
    Regional Headquarters,
    Exhibition Road,
    London, S.W.1.

Copy of memorandum by Regional Technical
Adviser

'G' BRANCH   RTA/BETH/TS/AC

Bethnal Green
Entrance to the Tube Shelter

I have again inspected the approach to this shelter and
I am still of the opinion that it would be a waste of
money to build up a wall round the steps to prevent
the crowd from forcing their way into the shelter, the
existing fence, with a little stiffening with salvaged
timber, could be made very much stronger than the
gate. If anything is at all likely to be forced it is the gate
which, I agree, might be stiffened with advantage.

On the other hand the proposal for a covering over
the entrance, now put forward for the first time in the
Town Clerkís letter of the 30th September, is I consider a necessity since, as things are at present during
wet weather, rain must pour down the approach
steps. I strongly doubt, however, if anything like 3 in.
of water could possibly ever collect on the first landing even after extremely heavy and continuous rain.
I have discussed this with the Deputy Borough
Engineer and he will, I understand, submit a proposal
for this cover over the entrance.

Regional Technical Adviser.
17th October, 1941.

Copy of London Region reply to Borough Council

Exhibition Road.
20th October, 1941

BETH/

With reference to your letter of the 30th September regarding the surround at the entrance to the Bethnal Green Tube Shelter, I am desired by the Regional Commissioners to say that they have further considered the matter in the light of a recent report by the Regional Technical Adviser, and they remain of the opinion that it is not necessary to remove the existing fencing and replace it by brick walling.

The Commissioners agree, however, that it is desirable to strengthen the gateway and they also agree to the covering over of the entrance stairway in order to prevent the rain flowing down the stairs into the shelter.

It is understood from the Regional Technical Adviser that these measures have been discussed with the Deputy Borough Engineer, and that plans for the above-mentioned works are now being prepared for submission to this Department in due course.

Town Clerk,
    Metropolitan Borough of Bethnal Green,
    Town Clerk's Office, Town Hall,
    Bethnal Green, E.2.

METROPOLITAN BOROUGH OF BETHNAL GREEN

Town Clerk's Office,
Town Hall,
Bethnal Green, E.2.
G/K   *24th October, 1941.*

Sir,

Bethnal Green Tube Shelter – Surround at Entrance

Your letter of the 20th instant has been considered by the General Emergency and Finance Committee, and I have to inform you that the Committee remains of the firm opinion that a brick wall surround at the entrance to the Bethnal Green Tube Shelter is necessary.

I am to point out that this facility has been granted in other Boroughs in similar circumstances, and to ask that you will be good enough to reconsider your decision in the matter.

I am, Sir,
Your obedient Servant,
(Sgd.) S. P. FERDINANDO.

The Chief Administrative Officer,
London Civil Defence Region,
Exhibition Road,
London, S.W.7.

Copy of minutes exchanged between "G" Branch, London Region, and Regional Technical Adviser.

Regional Technical Adviser.

re letter of 24/10

I take it that the opinion expressed in our letter of the 20th October still stands.

"G" Branch.
29/10/41

"G" Branch.

Yes, that is correct, but I agree that the walls supporting the roof over the steps may be of brickwork so that, in fact, the Bethnal Green Council will now get their original request, but for a different reason, i.e., for the purpose of supporting the roof.

Regional Technical Adviser.
1/11/41

Copy of London Region reply to Borough Council

Exhibition Road
18th November, 1941.

BETH/36

With reference to your letter (G/K) of the 24th October, regarding the surround at the entrance to the Bethnal Green Tube Shelter, I am directed by the Regional Commissioners to say that they have further considered the matter and that they see no reason to vary their previous decision. They are advised, however, that it is desirable to provide brick wall supports to the covering over the entrance to which approval was given by the Department's letter of the 20th October. As indicated therein, plans and estimates of costs of these works are awaited.

The Town Clerk,
    Metropolitan Borough of Bethnal Green,
    Town Hall,
    Bethnal Green, E.2.

IN MEMORY OF THE 173 MEN, WOMEN
AND CHILDREN WHO LOST THEIR LIVES
ON THE EVENING OF WEDNESDAY
3RD MARCH 1943 DESCENDING THESE
STEPS TO BETHNAL GREEN
UNDERGROUND
AIR RAID SHELTER.

NOT FORGOTTEN

*Words from the plaque in Bethnal Green underground
station commemorating those killed in the accident.*

Titles in the series

The Boer War: Ladysmith and Mafeking, 1900

The British Empire went to war against the Boers in South Africa in October 1899. Within a few weeks the two main British forces were besieged in the towns of Ladysmith and Mafeking, and a huge army was shipped from England to rescue them. These papers are the despatches to London from the commanders in the field.

"As regards the withdrawal of the troops from the Spion Kop position, which, though occupied almost without opposition in the early morning of the 24th January, had to be held throughout the day under an extremely heavy fire, and the retention of which had become essential to the relief of Ladysmith, I regret that I am unable to concur with Sir Redvers Buller in thinking that Lieut.-Colonel Thorneycroft exercised a wise discretion in ordering the troops to retire. Even admitting that the senior Officers on the summit of the hill might have been more promptly informed of the measures taken by Sir Charles Warren to support and rein-force them, I am of opinion that Lieut.-Colonel Thorneycroft's assumption of responsibility and authority was wholly inexcus-able. During the night the enemy's fire, if it did not cease altogether, could not have been formidable, and, though lamp signalling was not possible at the time, owing to the supply of oil having failed, it would not have taken more than two or three hours at most for Lieut.-Colonel Thorneycroft to communicate by messenger with Major-General Coke or Sir Charles Warren, and to receive a reply. Major-General Coke appears to have left Spion Kop at 9.30 p.m. for the purpose of consulting with Sir Charles Warren, and up to that hour the idea of a withdrawal had not been entertained. Yet almost immediately after Major-General Coke's departure Lieut.-Colonel Thorneycroft issued an order, without' reference to superior authority, which upset the whole plan of operations, and rendered unavailing the sacrifices which had already been made to carry it into effect."

ISBN 0 11 702408 2

Wilfrid Blunt's Egyptian Garden: Fox Hunting in Cairo

At the time of this correspondence Egypt had been in the protection of the British Empire since 1882. In 1900, in order to provide sport for the officers, a pack of hounds was shipped out from England to hunt the Egyptian fox.

Sir R. Rodd to the Marquess of Lansdowne. — (Received July 23.)

(Telegraphic)   Cairo, July 23, 1901

ON Sunday morning a fox-hunt was taking place near Cairo, in the desert, the hounds following a scent crossed the boundary-wall of Mr. Wilfrid Blunt's property, and two of the field, being British officers, who were acting as whips, went in to turn them back. Mr. Blunt's watchmen surrounded them, and, although they explained their intention, treated them with considerable violence. The senior officer present approached, and strictly forbade any attempt at retaliation. The overseer of the property helped in procuring the names of the aggressors. An inquiry is proceeding, and action will be taken against the chief offenders.

The officers were all dressed in mufti, and no special importance attaches itself to the matter, but it is necessary to show clearly that private servants in charge of landed property will not be permitted to use personal violence in order to prevent trespassing.

ISBN 0 11 702415 5

The British Invasion of Tibet: Colonel Younghusband, 1904

In 1903, a British Missionary Force under the leadership of Colonel Francis Younghusband crossed over the border from India and invaded Tibet. This is the account of his actions.

"23rd July, 1903. – Fine still morning. Some light clouds in the sky. Maximum temperature yesterday 67.8°; minimum last night 41°.

Colonel Younghusband and Mr. White rode out during the day to visit the Kozo hot spring, which lies in a valley some two or three miles north of Khamba Jong. They found the temperature of the hottest spring to be 175°F. A young Tibetan from the Chinese camp visited me in the evening, and I had an interesting conversation with him regarding Tibetan manners and customs. His elder brother is a monk in Sera monastery, and he tells me the monks of the three big monasteries are a truculent lot – regularly drilled, bitterly hostile to foreigners, and apparently spoiling for a fight. Arms of sorts for all the monks are stored in the monasteries. He tells me that the nominal number of monks in Sera – 5,500 – is far below the reality, and similarly in De-bung and Ga-den. He is the third brother of four, and the three younger have one wife between them. He explained a good many of the household arrangements, and I hope to get hold of him again and learn some more. He says Mr. Ho detests this place. The water doesn't agree with him, and he has a bucket (of the Tibetan pattern) of water brought to him daily from Giaogong, at a cost of 12 annas. Like all the poorer class of Tibetans he complains of the extortions of the officials in the matter of taxes and forced carriage (kar begar of the North-West). He says every penny we pay here for grass and so on goes into the pockets of the Jongpen, and nothing whatever reaches the wretched misser, or peasant."

ISBN 0 11 702409 0

The Strange Story of Adolph Beck

In 1895, Adolph Beck was arrested and convicted of the crimes of deception and larceny. The account given here is one of the strangest true stories in British legal history.

"I, Ada Wooding, live at 8, Northway Road, Cambrian Road, Brixton. I am single. About four months ago I met prisoner between Charing Cross and Ludgate Hill. We had a conversation and he said he should like to see me again. He came to my address on the 8th March after I had received a letter from him. He said he had an offer to make me, and my house was not good enough for me, and he would keep me. He had a villa at St. John's Wood and I was to go there and have a servant, a page, and a little trap to go out in. He brought out a cheque for £13 10s. and said I was too quiet, and I was to have different dresses and go for them to Howell and James. He would send his brougham for me between 6 and 7 o'clock, and I was to have some boxes and some jewellery. He also said my rings were not good enough. They were too thick and clumsy. He asked me to put them in an envelope and he would have a sapphire stone put in my wedding ring. The diamond ring was not good enough, and I put them in an envelope and let him take them because I believed the cheque to be good. He gave me the cheque before he took the jewellery. He said he'd broken one of his sleeve-links and would I let him have mine. I lent them to him. It was snowing. I said 'Will you have an umbrella?' and I lent him mine. He said he should like a cab but he had no money. I lent him 5s. He then went away. I never saw my jewellery again till to-day. They are now produced. I sent to Howell and James and to the Bank of London. I never saw him again until to-day.

Signed. ADA WOODING".

ISBN 0 11 702414 7